MW01168650

Mom, I Want to Hear Your Story

A Mother's
Guided Journal
To Share Her Life &
Her Love

Jeffrey Mason

"A MOTHER IS ALWAYS THE BEGINNING. SHE IS HOW THINGS BEGIN."

– ANONYMOUS

ABOUT THIS BOOK

Being a Mother is forever.

NO MATTER HOW OLD OR WHERE THEY ARE, YOUR CHILDREN
REMAIN ATTACHED TO YOU, YOUR LIVES FOREVER INTERWOVEN.
THEY ARE ALWAYS IN YOUR THOUGHTS AND HEARTS.

Being a Mother is constant.

WONDERING HOW YOUR CHILDREN ARE DOING IS ALWAYS A PART
OF YOU. EVEN AFTER THEY HAVE GROWN AND MOVED ON, YOUR SLEEP
REMAINS A LITTLE LESS RESTFUL, YOUR EARS STILL LISTENING FOR A
MIDNIGHT CRY FROM A CRIB THAT HAS BEEN GONE FOR YEARS.

Being a Mother is unconditional.

NO MATTER THE PATHS YOUR CHILDREN TRAVEL OR THE CHOICES THEY
MAKE, YOUR LOVE IS AS UNRELENTING AS THE DAY YOU FIRST HELD THEM.

Being a Mother is quiet.

YOUR CONSTANT SACRIFICE TO YOUR CHILDREN AND FAMILY
IS ALWAYS THERE BUT OFTEN UNSEEN. LIKE THE AIR AROUND US, A
MOTHER'S GIFT OF HERSELF IS PART OF EVERYTHING.

THIS BOOK WAS CREATED TO GIVE MOTHERS A PLACE TO SHARE
THE STORIES OF THEIR LIVES: WHAT THEY HAVE EXPERIENCED, THEIR
ACCOMPLISHMENTS, CHALLENGES, VICTORIES, AND DREAMS.

THE HOPE IS THAT THIS BOOK WILL CREATE CONVERSATIONS,
ENCOURAGE UNDERSTANDING, AND SERVE AS A REMINDER OF
ALL OUR MOMS HAVE GIVEN FOR US AND TO US

"Mother, the ribbons of your love are woven around my heart."
– Anonymous

THIS BOOK BELONGS TO:

_____

_____

IT'S YOUR BIRTHDAY!
"Life began with waking up and loving my mother's face."
— George Eliot

What is your birthdate?

_____

What was your full name at birth?

_____

Were you named after a relative or someone else of significance?

_____

_____

_____

_____

In what city were you born?

_____

What was your length and weight at birth?

_____

Were you born in a hospital? If not, where?

_____

_____

What were your first words?

_____

_____

IT'S YOUR BIRTHDAY!

"All that I am or ever hope to be, I owe to my angel mother."
— Abraham Lincoln

How old were you when you started to walk?

_____

How old were your parents when you were born?

_____

_____

How did your parents describe you as a baby?

_____

_____

_____

_____

_____

_____

_____

_____

_____

_____

IT'S YOUR BIRTHDAY!

*"The great use of life is to spend it for
something that will outlast it."* — William James

What stories have you been told about the day you were born?

_____

_____

_____

_____

_____

_____

_____

_____

_____

_____

_____

_____

_____

IT'S YOUR BIRTHDAY!

"A mother is she who can take the place of all others but whose place no one else can take." — Cardinal Meymillod

What is a favorite childhood memory?

_____

_____

_____

_____

_____

_____

_____

_____

_____

_____

_____

_____

_____

_____

_____

_____

WHAT HAPPENED
THE YEAR YOU WERE BORN?

"For the hand that rocks the cradle is the
hand that rules the world." — William Ross Wallace

Google the following for the year you were born:
What are some notable events that occurred?

_____

_____

_____

_____

_____

_____

What movie won the Academy Award for Best Picture? Who
won for Best Actor and Best Actress?

_____

_____

_____

What were a few popular movies that came out that year?

_____

_____

_____

_____

WHAT HAPPENED THE YEAR YOU WERE BORN?

"The most important thing in the
world is family and love." — John Wooden

What song was on the top of the Billboard charts?

_____

Who was the leader of the country (President, Prime
Minister, etc.)?

_____

What were a few popular television shows?

_____

_____

_____

_____

What were the prices for the following items?
- A loaf of bread:
- A gallon of milk:
- A cup of coffee:
- A dozen eggs:
- The average cost of a new home:
- A first-class stamp:
- A new car:
- A gallon of gas:
- A movie ticket:
- A movie ticket:

GROWING UP

"We are born of love; love is our mother."
— Rumi

How would you describe yourself when you were a kid?

_____

_____

_____

_____

_____

Did you have a nickname when you were growing up? If yes, how did you get it?

_____

Who were your best friends in your elementary school days? Are you still in contact with them?

_____

_____

_____

_____

What were your regular chores? Did you get an allowance? How much was it and what did you spend it on?

_____

_____

_____

GROWING UP
"Motherhood changes everything."
— Adriana Trigiani

Describe what your room looked like when you were growing up. Was it messy or clean? Did you have paintings or posters on the walls? What were the main colors?

_____

_____

_____

_____

_____

_____

_____

_____

What is one thing you miss about being a kid?

_____

_____

_____

_____

_____

MOM TRIVIA

"Of all the things my hands have held, the best, by far, is you."
— Author Unknown

What is your favorite flavor of ice cream?

_____

How do you like your coffee?

_____

_____

If you could live anywhere in the world for a year with all expenses paid, where would you choose?

_____

_____

_____

How do you like your eggs cooked?

_____

Preference: cook or clean?

_____

What is your shoe size?

_____

What superpower would you choose for yourself?

_____

_____

_____

MOM TRIVIA

"Life doesn't come with a manual; it comes with a mother."
— Author Unknown

Do you have any allergies?

_____

_____

_____

What is your biggest fear?

_____

_____

What would you order as your last meal?

_____

_____

_____

_____

Have you ever broken a bone? Which one(s) and how?

_____

_____

What is your favorite flower or plant?

_____

THE TEENAGE YEARS

"The scariest part of raising a teenager is remembering the things you did when you were a teenager." — Author Unknown

How would you describe yourself when you were a teenager?

_____

_____

_____

_____

How did you dress and style your hair during your teens?

_____

_____

_____

_____

Did you hang out with a group or just a few close friends? Are you still close with any of them?

_____

_____

_____

_____

THE TEENAGE YEARS

"Teenagehood – that time in life when you show your individuality by looking like everyone else." — Author Unknown

Describe a typical Friday or Saturday night during your high school years.

_____

_____

_____

_____

Did you have a curfew?

_____

Did you date during your high school years?

_____

_____

Did you go to any school dances? What were they like?

_____

_____

_____

_____

Who taught you to drive and in what kind of car?

_____

_____

THE TEENAGE YEARS
"Little children, headache; big children, heartache."
— Italian Proverb

How old were you when you got your first car? What kind of car was it (year, make, and model)?

_____

_____

What school activities or sports did you participate in?

_____

_____

_____

_____

_____

What did you like and dislike about high school?

_____

_____

_____

_____

_____

_____

THE TEENAGE YEARS

"Keep true to the dreams of your youth."
— Friedrich Schiller

What were your grades like?

_____

_____

Did you have a favorite subject and a least favorite?

_____

_____

_____

_____

What are a few favorite songs from your high school years?

_____

_____

_____

_____

_____

_____

_____

_____

THE TEENAGE YEARS
"Having a teenager can cause parents to wonder
about each other's heredity." — Author Unknown

Knowing all you know now, what advice would you give to
your teenage self? What might you have done differently in
school if you knew then what you know now?

_____

_____

_____

_____

_____

_____

_____

_____

_____

_____

_____

_____

_____

_____

THE TEENAGE YEARS

"Life is a winding path through hills and valleys and in
the end, the journey is all that matters." — Author Unknown

Write about a teacher, coach, or other mentor who had a
significant impact on you when you were growing up.

_____

_____

_____

_____

_____

_____

_____

_____

_____

_____

_____

_____

_____

_____

_____

BEGINNINGS

"We don't stop going to school when we graduate."
— Carol Burnett

What did you do after high school? Did you get a job, serve in the military, go to college or a trade school? Something else?

_____

_____

_____

_____

_____

Why did you make this choice?

_____

_____

_____

_____

_____

If you went to college or trade school, what was your major/the focus of your education?

_____

_____

_____

BEGINNINGS
"it takes courage to grow up and become who you really are"
— ee cummings

How did this time period impact who you are today?

_____

_____

_____

_____

_____

If you could go back, what, if anything, would you change about this period of your life? Why?

_____

_____

_____

_____

_____

_____

_____

_____

WORK & CAREER

"Even if you're on the right track, you'll get
run over if you just sit there." — Will Rogers

When you were a kid, what did you want to be when you grew up?

_____

_____

What was your first job? How old were you? How much were you paid?

_____

_____

How many jobs have you had during your lifetime? List a few of your favorites.

_____

_____

_____

_____

_____

What is the least favorite job you have had?

_____

_____

_____

WORK & CAREER

"I'm a great believer in luck, and I find the harder
I work, the more I have of it." — Thomas Jefferson

Is there a job or profession your parents wanted you to
pursue? What was it?

_____

_____

_____

_____

When people ask what profession you are/were in, your
response is...

_____

_____

_____

How did you get into this career?

_____

_____

_____

_____

_____

_____

WORK & CAREER
"Choose a job you love and you will never
have to work a day in your life." — Confucius

What are/were the best parts of this profession?

_____

_____

_____

_____

_____

_____

_____

What aspects did you or do you dislike about it?

_____

_____

_____

_____

_____

_____

_____

WORK & CAREER

"If people knew how hard I worked to get my mastery,
it wouldn't seem so wonderful after all." — Michelangelo

Who was the best boss you ever had? Why were they such a good manager?

_____

_____

_____

_____

_____

What are some of your work and career-related achievements that you are proudest of?

_____

_____

_____

_____

_____

_____

_____

MOM TRIVIA

"Before I got married, I had six theories about raising
children; now, I have six children and no theories." — John Wilmot

Have you ever been told that you look like someone
famous? If yes, who?

_____

_____

_____

What is your morning routine?

_____

_____

_____

_____

What is a favorite guilty pleasure?

_____

_____

_____

_____

Which television family most reminds you of your family?

_____

_____

MOM TRIVIA

"Mothers hold their children's hands for a short
while, but their hearts forever." — Author Unknown

Did you have braces? If yes, how old were you when you
got them?

_____

Do you like roller coasters?

_____

_____

What name would you choose if you had to change your
first name?

_____

_____

Did you ever skip school?

_____

_____

If yes, did you get away with it and what did you do during
the time you should have been in class?

_____

_____

_____

_____

_____

FAMILY TREE
"Each of us is tomorrow's ancestors."
— Author Unknown

My Great-Grandmother
(My Grandmother's Mom)

My Great-Grandmothe
(My Grandfather's Mom

My Great-Grandfather
(My Grandmother's Dad)

My Great-Grandfather
(My Grandfather's Dad

My Grandmother
(My Mom's Mom)

My Grandfather
(My Mom's Dad)

My Mother

FAMILY TREE

"As you do for your ancestors, your children will do for you."
— African Proverb

My Great-Grandmother
(My Grandmother's Mom)

My Great-Grandmother
(My Grandfather's Mom)

My Great-Grandfather
(My Grandmother's Dad)

My Great-Grandfather
(My Grandfather's Dad)

My Grandmother
(My Dad's Mom)

My Grandfather
(My Dad's Dad)

My Father

PARENTS & GRANDPARENTS

"If evolution really works, how come
mothers only have two hands?" — Milton Berle

Where was your mother born and where did she grow up?

_____

_____

_____

What three words would you use to describe her?

_____

_____

_____

In what ways are you most like your mother?

_____

_____

_____

_____

_____

_____

_____

_____

PARENTS & GRANDPARENTS

"You will never look back on life and think, 'I
spent too much time with my kids.'" — Author Unknown

Where was your father born and where did he grow up?

_____

_____

_____

What three words would you use to describe him?

_____

_____

_____

In what ways are you most like your father?

_____

_____

_____

_____

_____

_____

_____

_____

PARENTS & GRANDPARENTS

"A moment lasts for seconds but the memory of it lasts forever."
— Author Unknown

What is a favorite memory of your mother?

_____

_____

_____

_____

_____

_____

_____

_____

_____

_____

_____

_____

PARENTS & GRANDPARENTS

"We don't remember days, we remember moments."
— Author Unknown

What is a favorite memory of your father?

_____

_____

_____

_____

_____

_____

_____

_____

_____

_____

_____

_____

_____

_____

_____

_____

PARENTS & GRANDPARENTS

"To forget one's ancestors is to be a brook without
a source, a tree without a root." — Chinese Proverb

What was your mother's maiden name?

_____

Do you know from what part(s) of the world your mother's
family originates?

_____

_____

_____

Do you know your father's mother's maiden name?

_____

_____

Do you know from what part(s) of the world your father's
family originates?

_____

_____

_____

How did your parents meet?

_____

_____

_____

_____

PARENTS & GRANDPARENTS

"Appreciate your parents. You never know what
sacrifices they went through for you." — Author Unknown

How would you describe their relationship?

_____

_____

_____

_____

_____

What were your parents' occupations?

_____

_____

_____

Did either of them have any unique talents or skills?

_____

_____

_____

_____

Did either of them serve in the military?

_____

_____

PARENTS & GRANDPARENTS

"Love is the chain whereby to bind a child to its parents."
— Abraham Lincoln

What is a favorite family tradition that was passed down from your parents or grandparents?

_____

_____

_____

_____

What are a few of your favorite things that your mother or father would cook for the family?

_____

_____

_____

_____

What were your grandparents like on your mother's side?

_____

_____

_____

_____

PARENTS & GRANDPARENTS
"Next to God, thy parents."
— William Penn

Where were your mother's parents born and grow up?

_____

_____

_____

_____

What were your grandparents like on your father's side?

_____

_____

_____

_____

_____

_____

Where were your father's parents born and grow up?

_____

_____

_____

_____

PARENTS & GRANDPARENTS

"There is no school equal to a decent home and no
teacher equal to a virtuous parent." — Mahatma Gandhi

What is some of the best advice your mother gave you?

_____

_____

_____

_____

_____

_____

_____

_____

_____

_____

_____

_____

_____

_____

_____

PARENTS & GRANDPARENTS

"A father's goodness is higher than the mountain,
a mother's goodness deeper than the sea." — Japanese Proverb

What is some of the best advice your father gave you?

_____

_____

_____

_____

_____

_____

_____

_____

_____

_____

_____

_____

_____

_____

_____

_____

PARENTS & GRANDPARENTS

"My fathers planted for me, and I planted for my children."
— Hebrew Saying

Did you ever meet your great-grandparents on either side of your family? If yes, what were they like?

_____

_____

_____

_____

_____

_____

_____

_____

_____

_____

_____

_____

PARENTS & GRANDPARENTS
"The longest road out is the shortest road home."
— Irish Proverb

What other individuals had a major role in helping you grow up?

_____

_____

_____

_____

_____

_____

_____

_____

_____

_____

_____

_____

_____

_____

YOUR SIBLINGS

"Brothers and sisters are as close as hands and feet."
— Vietnamese Saying

Are you an only child, or do you have siblings?

_____

_____

Are you the oldest, middle, or youngest?

_____

_____

List your siblings' names in order of their ages. Make sure to include yourself.

_____

_____

_____

_____

_____

_____

Which of your siblings were you the closest with growing up?

_____

_____

_____

Which of your siblings are you the closest with in your adult years?

_____

_____

_____

YOUR SIBLINGS

"The greatest gift our parents ever gave us was each other."
— Author Unknown

How would you describe each of your siblings when they were kids?

_____

_____

_____

_____

_____

_____

_____

How would you describe each of your siblings as adults?

_____

_____

_____

_____

_____

_____

_____

YOUR SIBLINGS

"First a brother, then a bother, now a friend."
— Author Unknown

In the following pages, share some favorite memories of each of your siblings. If you're an only child, feel free to share memories of close friends or cousins.

_____

_____

_____

_____

_____

_____

_____

_____

_____

_____

_____

_____

_____

YOUR SIBLINGS

"What causes sibling rivalry? Having more than one kid."
— Tim Allen

Memories...

_____

_____

_____

_____

_____

_____

_____

_____

_____

_____

_____

_____

_____

_____

_____

YOUR SIBLINGS

"Siblings know how to push each other's buttons, but they also know how to mend things faster than anyone." — Author Unknown

Memories...

_____

_____

_____

_____

_____

_____

_____

_____

_____

_____

_____

_____

_____

YOUR SIBLINGS

"The advantage of growing up with siblings is that
you become very good at fractions." — Author Unknown

Memories...

_____

_____

_____

_____

_____

_____

_____

_____

_____

_____

_____

_____

_____

_____

"GOD COULD NOT BE EVERYWHERE, AND THEREFORE HE CREATED MOTHERS."

- JEWISH PROVERB

"MOTHERHOOD: ALL LOVE BEGINS AND ENDS THERE."
- ROBERT BROWNING

BECOMING & BEING A MOM

*"My mother had a great deal of trouble with
me, but I think she enjoyed it."* — Mark Twain

How old were you when you first became a mother?

_____

What was your favorite part about being pregnant?

_____

_____

_____

_____

_____

_____

What difficulties did you have with your pregnancies, if any?

_____

_____

_____

_____

_____

BECOMING & BEING A MOM

"Being a mom is the answer to every question. She is our why, who, what and when." — Author Unknown

Were your deliveries early, late, or on-time?

_____

_____

_____

_____

Did you have any food cravings? If yes, what were they?

_____

_____

_____

_____

_____

What were your children's lengths and weights at birth?

_____

_____

_____

_____

BECOMING & BEING A MOM

"Sweater, n. garment worn by a child when
its mother is feeling chilly." — Ambrose Bierce

Is there a special song you would sing or play to your children when they were little?

_____

_____

_____

How did having children impact your professional life?

_____

_____

_____

_____

What are the biggest differences in how kids are raised today and when you were young?

_____

_____

_____

_____

_____

BECOMING & BEING A MOM

"A man's work is from sun to sun, but
a mother's work is never done." — Author Unknown

Looking back, what would you change about how your kids were brought up, if anything?

_____

_____

_____

_____

_____

_____

_____

_____

_____

_____

_____

_____

_____

_____

BECOMING & BEING A MOM

"There is no greater name for a leader than mother or father. There is no leadership more important than parenthood." — Sheri L. Dew

What are the best and hardest parts of being a mother?

_____

_____

_____

_____

_____

_____

_____

_____

_____

_____

_____

_____

_____

_____

_____

_____

BECOMING & BEING A MOM

"The mother is the highest asset of national life; more important than the statesman, or businessman, artist, or scientist." — Theodore Roosevelt

Write about a favorite memory of being a mother.

BECOMING & BEING A MOM

"Pretty much all the honest truth telling there is in
the world is done by children." — Oliver Wendell Holmes

Knowing what you know now, what advice would you give
yourself as a new mom?

_____

_____

_____

_____

_____

_____

_____

_____

_____

_____

_____

_____

BECOMING & BEING A MOM

"Becoming a mother makes you realize you
can do almost anything one-handed." — Author Unknown

Based upon all you have learned and experienced, what
advice would you give your children?

_____

_____

_____

_____

_____

_____

_____

_____

_____

_____

_____

_____

LET'S TALK ABOUT YOUR KIDS

"The best academy is a mother's knee."— James Russell Lowell

What would your kids have been named if they were born the opposite gender?

_____

_____

_____

_____

Who did they most look like when they were babies?

_____

_____

_____

_____

_____

What were their first words?

_____

_____

_____

_____

LET'S TALK ABOUT YOUR KIDS
"The longest road out is the shortest road home." — Irish Proverb

How old were they when they took their first steps?

_____

_____

_____

Were any of your children "surprises?"

_____

_____

_____

Are there any specific books you remember reading to your kids?

_____

_____

_____

When your kids were little, what trick did you use to calm them when they were upset?

_____

_____

_____

_____

LET'S TALK ABOUT YOUR KIDS
"Adults are just outdated children."
— Dr. Seuss

In what ways are your kids like you?

_____

_____

_____

_____

_____

_____

_____

_____

_____

_____

_____

_____

_____

_____

LET'S TALK ABOUT YOUR KIDS

"Hugs can do great amounts of good, especially for children."
— Diana, Princess of Wales

How are they different?

_____

_____

_____

_____

_____

_____

_____

_____

_____

_____

_____

_____

_____

MOM TRIVIA

"Biology is the least of what makes someone a mother."
— Oprah Winfrey

If you could do any one thing for a day, what would it be?

_____

_____

_____

What is your favorite season? What are some things you love about that time of the year?

_____

_____

_____

What is a smell that reminds you of your childhood? Why?

_____

_____

_____

What is your least favorite household chore?

_____

_____

What do you do better than anyone else in the family?

_____

_____

MOM TRIVIA

"I was always at peace because of the way my mom treated me."
— Martina Hingis

What is your favorite dessert?

_____

_____

What is a favorite memory from the last twelve months?

_____

_____

_____

_____

If you could only eat three things for the next year (with no effect on your health), what would you pick?

_____

_____

_____

What is your definition of success?

_____

_____

_____

_____

_____

SPIRITUALITY & RELIGION

"I love my mother as trees love water and sunshine. She helps me grow, prosper, and reach great heights." — Author Unknown

What do you believe is the purpose of life?

_____

_____

_____

_____

_____

_____

Which has the most impact on our lives: fate or free will?

_____

_____

_____

_____

_____

_____

SPIRITUALITY & RELIGION

"When you feel neglected, think of the female salmon who lays 3,000,000 eggs but is forgotten on Mother's Day." — Sam Ewing

Were your parents religious when you were growing up? How did they express their spiritual beliefs?

_____

_____

_____

_____

_____

_____

_____

_____

_____

_____

_____

_____

_____

SPIRITUALITY & RELIGION

"If you bungle raising your children, I don't think whatever
else you do will matter very much." — Jacqueline Kennedy Onassis

If you are religious or spiritual, how have your beliefs and
practices changed over the course of your life?

_____

_____

_____

_____

_____

_____

_____

_____

_____

_____

_____

_____

SPIRITUALITY & RELIGION

"What you are is God's gift to you, what you become
is your gift to God." — Hans Urs von Balthasar, *Prayer*

What religious or spiritual practices do you incorporate into
your daily life today, if any?

_____

_____

_____

_____

_____

_____

_____

Do you believe in miracles? Have you experienced one?

_____

_____

_____

_____

_____

SPIRITUALITY & RELIGION

"Within you there is a stillness and a sanctuary to which
you can retreat at any time and be yourself." — Hermann Hesse

What do you do when times are challenging, and you need
to find additional inner strength?

_____

_____

_____

_____

_____

_____

_____

_____

_____

_____

_____

_____

_____

SPIRITUALITY & RELIGION

"Families are like branches on a tree. We grow in different directions, yet our roots remain as one." — Author Unknown

Write about a time you found relief by forgiving someone.

_____

_____

_____

_____

_____

_____

_____

_____

_____

_____

_____

_____

_____

_____

LOVE & ROMANCE
"We are asleep until we fall in love!"
— Leo Tolstoy, *War and Peace*

Do you believe in love at first sight?

_____

_____

_____

Do you believe in soulmates?

_____

_____

_____

How old were you when you had your first kiss?

_____

What age were you when you went on your first date?

_____

Can you remember who it was with and what you did?

_____

_____

_____

_____

LOVE & ROMANCE

"Whatever our souls are made of, his and mine are the same."
— Emily Brontë, *Wuthering Heights*

How old were you when you had your first steady relationship? Who was it with?

_____

How many times in your life have you been in love?

_____

_____

What are some of the most important qualities of a successful relationship?

_____

_____

_____

_____

_____

_____

_____

LOVE & ROMANCE

"We loved with a love that was more than love."
— Edgar Allan Poe, *Annabel Lee*

Did you have any celebrity crushes when you were young?

_____

_____

_____

Were you ever in a relationship with someone your parents did not approve of?

_____

_____

_____

Have you ever written someone or had someone write you a love poem or song?

_____

If yes, write a few lines that you may remember.

_____

_____

_____

_____

_____

LOVE & ROMANCE
"Love is a great beautifier."
— Louisa May Alcott, *Little Women*

In what ways do you feel your parents' relationship influenced how you have approached love and marriage?

_____

_____

_____

_____

_____

_____

Write about a favorite romantic moment.

_____

_____

_____

_____

_____

_____

_____

LOVE & ROMANCE
"We don't remember days, we remember moments."
— Author Unknown

How did you meet our Dad?

_____

_____

_____

_____

_____

What was your first impression of him?

_____

_____

_____

_____

_____

What is your proposal story?

_____

_____

_____

_____

_____

LOVE & ROMANCE
"Children are the hands by which we take hold of heaven."
— Henry Ward Beecher

What was your wedding like? Where was it held and who was there? Any good wedding day stories?

_____

_____

_____

_____

_____

_____

_____

_____

_____

_____

_____

_____

_____

TRAVEL

"Once a year, go someplace you've never been before."
— Dali Lama

Do you have a valid passport?

_____

How do you feel about cruises?

_____

_____

How do you feel about flying?

_____

_____

What are a few of your favorite places you have traveled to?

_____

_____

_____

_____

_____

_____

_____

_____

TRAVEL

"Life is short, and the world is wide."
— Author Unknown

What is a favorite travel memory?

_____

_____

_____

_____

_____

_____

_____

_____

_____

_____

_____

_____

_____

TRAVEL BUCKET LIST

"Man cannot discover new oceans unless he has
the courage to lose sight of the shore." — André Gide

List the top 10 places you would visit if money and time
were no concern.

1. _____

   _____

2. _____

   _____

3. _____

   _____

4. _____

   _____

5. _____

   _____

TRAVEL BUCKET LIST

"The world is a book, and those who do not
travel read only one page." — Saint Augustine

6. _____

_____

7. _____

_____

8. _____

_____

9. _____

_____

10. _____

_____

"A MOTHER'S ARMS
ARE MADE OF TENDERNESS
AND CHILDREN SLEEP
SOUNDLY IN THEM."

- VICTOR HUGO

"CHILDREN ARE THE
ANCHORS THAT HOLD A
MOTHER TO LIFE."

- SOPHOCLES

MOM TRIVIA
"I really learned it all from mothers."
— Benjamin Spock

What would you title your autobiography?

_____

_____

_____

Do you think you could still pass the written portion of the driver's test without studying?

_____

What is your favorite color?

_____

What is your favorite quote?

_____

_____

_____

Do you believe in life on other planets?

_____

_____

If you could travel through time and had to choose, who would you meet: your ancestors or your descendants?

_____

_____

MOM TRIVIA
"My daughter introduced me to myself."
— Beyoncé Knowles

What personal accomplishments are you most proud of?

_____

_____

_____

_____

_____

_____

What are five things you are grateful for?

_____

_____

_____

_____

_____

If you were forced to sing karaoke, what song would you perform?

_____

_____

POLITICAL STUFF
"What you teach your children, you also teach their children."
— Author Unknown

Which best describes how you feel about having political discussions:

☐ I would rather not.

☐ I prefer to have them with people whose views match mine.

☐ I love a good debate.

How old were you the first time you voted?

_____

What are the biggest differences in your political views today and when you were in your early twenties?

_____

_____

_____

_____

_____

Have you ever taken part in a march or boycott? What issues, if any, could motivate you to join one?

_____

_____

_____

POLITICAL STUFF
"In politics stupidity is not a handicap."
— Napoleon Bonaparte

When was the last time you voted?

_____

In what ways do you agree and disagree with the political choices of your children's generation?

_____

_____

_____

_____

_____

If you woke up to find yourself in charge of the country, what are the first three things you would enact or change?

One:

_____

_____

Two:

_____

_____

Three:

_____

_____

MOVIES, MUSIC, TELEVISION, & BOOKS

"If you want a happy ending, that depends, of course, on where you stop your story." — Orson Welles

What movie have you watched the greatest number of times?

_____

_____

What movie or television show can you remember loving when you were a kid?

_____

_____

_____

Who would you cast to play yourself in the movie of your life? How about for the rest of your family?

_____

_____

_____

_____

_____

_____

_____

MOVIES, MUSIC, TELEVISION, & BOOKS

"Mom – the person most likely to write an autobiography and never mention herself." — Robert Breault

What are your favorite genres of music?

_____

_____

_____

_____

Which decades had the best music?

_____

_____

_____

_____

What is the first record (or cassette, cd, etc.) you can remember buying or being given as a gift?

_____

_____

What song do you like today that would make your younger self cringe?

_____

_____

MOVIES, MUSIC, TELEVISION, & BOOKS

"A mother is not a person to lean on, but a person
to make leaning unnecessary." — Dorothy Canfield Fisher

What is a song from your teens that reminds you of a special event or moment?

_____

_____

_____

What song would you pick as the theme song of your life?

_____

_____

What was the first concert you attended? Where was it held and when?

_____

_____

How has your taste in music changed over the years?

_____

_____

_____

_____

MOVIES, MUSIC, TELEVISION, & BOOKS

"Being a mother means that your heart is no longer yours;
it wanders wherever your children do." — George Bernard Shaw

What television show from the past do you wish was still on the air?

_____

If you could be cast in any television show or movie, past or present, which one would you choose?

_____

What are some favorite books from your childhood and/or teenage years?

_____

_____

_____

_____

What book or books have majorly impacted the way you think, work, or live your life?

_____

_____

_____

_____

_____

TOP TEN MOVIES
"Children need models rather than critics."
— Joseph Joubert

List up to ten of your most favorite movies:

1. _____

2. _____

3. _____

4. _____

5. _____

6. _____

7. _____

8. _____

9. _____

10. _____

TOP TEN SONGS

"The music is not in the notes, but in the silence in between." —
Wolfgang Amadeus Mozart

List up to ten of your most favorite songs:

1. _____

2. _____

3. _____

4. _____

5. _____

6. _____

7. _____

8. _____

9. _____

10. _____

MOM TRIVIA
"Mother's Day is the reason Alexander Graham
Bell invented the telephone." — Author Unknown

What is your favorite holiday and why?

_____

_____

_____

_____

_____

Is there anything in your family's medical history that your
kids should know about?

_____

_____

_____

_____

Which ten-year period of your life has been your favorite so
far and why?

_____

_____

_____

_____

MOM TRIVIA

"For when a child is born the mother is born again."
— Gilbert Parker

Who would you invite if you could have dinner with any five people who have ever lived?

_____

_____

_____

_____

_____

What are some of your most favorite books?

_____

_____

_____

_____

_____

_____

_____

_____

_____

ROOM FOR MORE

"Children are everything adults wish they could be."
— Author Unknown

The following pages are for you to expand on some of your answers, to share more memories, and/or to write notes to your loved ones:

_____

_____

_____

_____

_____

_____

_____

_____

_____

_____

_____

_____

_____

ROOM FOR MORE

"Children are apt to live up to what you believe of them."
— Lady Bird Johnson

_____

_____

_____

_____

_____

_____

_____

_____

_____

_____

_____

_____

_____

ROOM FOR MORE

"When you have brought up kids, there are memories
you store directly in your tear ducts." — Robert Brault

_____

_____

_____

_____

_____

_____

_____

_____

_____

_____

_____

_____

_____

_____

ROOM FOR MORE

"Children are like wet cement: whatever
falls on them makes an impression." — Haim Ginott

ROOM FOR MORE
"A mother understands what a child does not say."
— Author Unknown

_____

_____

_____

_____

_____

_____

_____

_____

_____

_____

_____

_____

_____

_____

_____

ROOM FOR MORE

"The soul is healed by being with children."
— Fyodor Dostoevsky

ROOM FOR MORE

"Without music, life would be a blank to me."
— Jane Austen

_____

_____

_____

_____

_____

_____

_____

_____

_____

_____

_____

_____

_____

_____

ROOM FOR MORE
"Music is the shorthand of emotion."
— Leo Tolstoy

_____

_____

_____

_____

_____

_____

_____

_____

_____

_____

_____

_____

_____

_____

HEAR YOUR STORY BOOKS

At **Hear Your Story**, we have created a line of books focused on giving each of us a place to tell the unique story of who we are, where we have been, and where we are going.

Sharing and hearing the stories of the people in our lives creates a closeness and understanding, ultimately strengthening our bonds.

Available at Amazon, all bookstores, and HearYourStoryBooks.com

- Mom, I Want to Hear Your Story: A Mother's Guided Journal to Share Her Life & Her Love

- Dad, I Want to Hear Your Story: A Father's Guided Journal to Share His Life & His Love

- Grandfather, I Want to Hear Your Story: A Grandfather's Guided Journal to Share His Life and His Love

- Tell Your Life Story: The Write Your Own Autobiography Guided Journal

- Life Gave Me You; I Want to Hear Your Story: A Guided Journal for Stepmothers to Share Their Life Story

- You Choose to Be My Dad; I Want to Hear Your Story: A Guided Journal for Stepdads to Share Their Life Story

HEAR YOUR STORY BOOKS

- To My Wonderful Aunt, I Want to Hear Your Story: A Guided Journal to Share Her Life and Her Love

- To My Uncle, I Want to Hear Your Story: A Guided Journal to Share His Life and His Love

- Mom, I Want to Learn Your Recipes: A Keepsake Memory Book to Gather and Preserve Your Favorite Family Recipes

- Dad, I Want to Learn Your Recipes: A Keepsake Memory Book to Gather and Preserve Your Favorite Family Recipes

- Grandmother, I Want to Learn Your Recipes: A Keepsake Memory Book to Gather and Preserve Your Favorite Family Recipes

- Grandfather, I Want to Learn Your Recipes: A Keepsake Memory Book to Gather and Preserve Your Favorite Family Recipes

- Aunt, I Want to Learn Your Recipes: A Keepsake Memory Book to Gather and Preserve Your Favorite Family Recipes

- Uncle, I Want to Learn Your Recipes: A Keepsake Memory Book to Gather and Preserve Your Favorite Family Recipes

- To My Girlfriend, I Want to Hear Your Story

- To My Boyfriend, I Want to Hear Your Story

- Mom & Me: Let's Learn Together Journal for Kids

DEDICATION

To Donna Niles Mason

My Mom

You are the strongest person I will ever know.
Your love, your spirit, and your fierce determination
gave me life, helped me become who I am, and remain
the lessons of my lifetime.

Thank you for your example and your love.

I Love You Mom

ABOUT THE AUTHOR

Jeffrey Mason is the creator and author of the best-selling **Hear Your Story®** line of books and is the founder of the company **Hear Your Story®**.

In response to his own father's fight with Alzheimer's, Jeffrey wrote his first two books, **Mom, I Want to Hear Your Story** and **Dad, I Want to Hear Your Story** in 2019. Since then, he has written and designed over 30 books, been published in four languages, and sold over 300,000 copies worldwide.

Jeffrey is dedicated to spreading the mission that the little things are the big things and that each of us has an incredible life story that needs to be shared and celebrated. He continues to create books that he hopes will guide people to reflect on and share their full life experience, while creating opportunities for talking, listening, learning, and understanding.

Hear Your Story® can be visited at **hearyourstorybooks.com** and Jeffrey can be contacted for questions, comments, podcasting, speaking engagements, or just a hello at **jeffrey.mason@hearyourstory.com**.

He would be grateful if you would help people find his books by leaving a review on Amazon. Your feedback helps him get better at this thing he loves.

VIEW THIS BOOK
ON YOUR COMPUTER

We invite you to also check out HearYourStory.com, where you can answer the questions in this book using your smart phone, tablet, or computer.

Answering the questions online at HearYourStory.com allows you to write as much as you want, to save your responses and revisit and revise them whenever you wish, and to print as many copies as you need for you and your whole family.

Please note there is a small one-time charge to cover the cost of maintaining the site.

ISBN: 978-1-955034-08-1

Made in the USA
Las Vegas, NV
30 April 2025

5940764e-1e06-4b5f-9049-f07a03b59ff3R01